From May Sarton's Well

From May Sarton's Well

Writings of May Sarton

Selection and Photographs by Edith Royce Schade

Papier-Mache Press
Watsonville, CA

First Edition

ISBN: 0-918949-51-3 Softcover
ISBN: 0-918949-52-1 Hardcover

Cover art by Edith Royce Schade
Cover design by Cynthia Heier
Photographs by Edith Royce Schade
Back cover photo of Edith Royce Schade by Gerhard Schade
Typesetting by Prism Photographics

Text used by permission of the author and W. W. Norton and Company, Inc., or the original publisher.
Grateful acknowledgment is made to Martha Wheelock, Ishtar Films, for permission to quote from the film *World of Light: A Portrait of May Sarton*.

Library of Congress Cataloging-in-Publication Data

Sarton, May, 1912-
    From May Sarton's well : writings of May Sarton / selection and photographs by Edith Royce Schade. — 1st ed.
        p.   cm.
    Includes bibliographical references.
    ISBN 0-918949-52-1 (acid-free paper) : $20.00. — ISBN 0-918949-51-3 (softcover : acid-free paper) : $12.00
    1. Sarton, May, 1912-   —Quotations.   2. Sarton, May, 1912—Illustrations.   3. Women—New England—Poetry.   4. Nature—Poetry.
    I. Schade, Edith Royce, 1937-   II. Title.
    PS3537.A832A6   1994
    811'.52—dc20   94-34507
                                                                  CIP

Dedication

This book is an anthology of work by May Sarton and a collection of the contributions of many people who have helped me directly and indirectly. I want to acknowledge these people, and I dedicate the book to them: to my husband, Gerhard, and sons Eric and Nick, for their support and patience; to my mother, Margaret N. Royce, my late father, Frank A. Royce, and my sisters, Margot, Bobbin, and Jan, for their nurturing; and of most of all to May Sarton, who is the core of this volume.

I want to thank Anne Alvord for her invitation and prodding which set me on this journey, Chet Wetzel and Sue Newman for their constructive criticism of my writing and editing, and Betty Daniel for proofreading the manuscript before I submitted it for publication. I extend my gratitude to Eric Swenson of W. W. Norton, who first expressed interest in the book and later helped me with the permissions process. I wish to thank Peri Aston of Wimbledon, London, England, for permission to use a montage photograph I made of her during her production of "Dance of the Woman Warrior." Final thanks go to Sandra Haldeman Martz, publisher, and all the rest of the staff at Papier-Mache Press for their help and kindness, and for being the kind of people who renew one's faith that there are still idealistic human beings in the publishing world.

Contents

From May Sarton's Well

Preface

A Glass of Water

Here is a glass of water from my well.
It tastes of rock and root and earth and rain;
It is the best I have, my only spell,
And it is cold, and better than champagne.
Perhaps someone will pass this house one day
To drink, and be restored, and go his way,
Someone in dark confusion as I was
When I drank down cold water in a glass,
Drank a transparent health to keep me sane,
After the bitter mood had gone again.
　　　　　—May Sarton

I first drank from May Sarton's well in 1971, when my mother gave me Sarton's memoir, *Plant Dreaming Deep*. There are now forty-three volumes of her work in my personal library. Most are dog-eared, especially the memoirs, journals, and poetry. An index card file box is stuffed with favorite quotations.

The intimate style of Sarton's journals made me feel like her personal friend, even before I had the remarkable good fortune of actually becoming one. I often find myself carrying on an imaginary conversation with her. The occasions when I am able to talk with her in person are always memorable.

Among Sarton's friends are literary greats, aspiring writers, students, artists, theater people, gardeners, photographers, and ordinary people. I am in the latter two categories. She is a muse to my creative photography and a guru for my *self*.

In 1980, my friend Anne Alvord invited me to join her in giving a talk on May Sarton's work for a program at our town's public library. Our audience's enthusiastic response led us to write to May, and also brought us more invitations to speak. As we prepared for our presentations, more correspondence emerged.

I found Sarton's imagery, particularly in her poetry, an inspiration for me when creating photographs, and discovered that many of my photographs already related to pieces of her writing. So my part in those lectures was as a photographer, showing projected slides which reflected on Sarton's work that Anne and I discussed.

I also began work on an exhibit of my prints which I paired with Sarton's poems and quotations. When I wrote to May about my plans for such an exhibit, she invited me to bring my photographs to her home so we could discuss them. That was in 1983—the beginning of our friendship. As my collection of quotes grew and the exhibition became a reality, a dream of doing a book began to crystallize. May's encouragement spurred me on.

In reading and rereading Sarton's books I found her influence on my life deepening. She helped me understand the struggle between my creative needs and the demands of my identities as a mother, wife, and member of the human race. At the end of the eloquent film, *World of Light: A Portrait of May Sarton* (which was later made into the book, *May Sarton—A Self Portrait*), May is asked what she most wants to be remembered for. She answers, "For being fully human."

Sarton's humanity, full of much strength and some foibles, sharing joys and sorrows, resonates through her writing. In selecting only some of her poems and excerpts of her prose, I feel the weight of tremendous responsibility. I have chosen pieces of her work which have great meaning to me; every person would make their own unique selections. And though it is possible that in pulling a quotation out of its original context, its meaning might seem to change, I believe that the inherent truth of her words remains. I think many readers will want to delve into more of Sarton's books after finishing this volume.

For the framework of this book, I have chosen a quotation which Sarton herself used as the theme for some of her poetry readings: "The delights of the poet as I jotted them down turned out to be light, solitude, the natural world, love, time, creation itself." Each of these delights forms a section in this book. The Afterword contains some of my pictures of, and thoughts about, the poet and her home in Maine.

I think of my photographs as an accompaniment to May's prose and poetry, as a piano is to a lyric singer—sometimes in unison, often in harmony, occasionally in counterpoint. Generally, I have paired my photographs with May's prose, separating the images from the poems so that the poetry may stand on its own as a point of departure for the reader's musings.

Sarton writes that the water from her well "tastes of rock and root and earth and rain." Although she does not think of herself as a "nature poet," she derives much enjoyment and inspiration as well as many metaphors from the natural world. Thus it seems right to me that the majority of my photographs capture images from nature, even when Sarton is speaking about people.

I hope you will "drink and be restored" by my photographs and Sarton's words, and share in my belief that we humans are the one species of animal which controls the fate of our fragile planet, and so bear the responsibility to cherish and care for it.

Light

For Monet

Poets, too, are crazed by light,
How to capture its changes,
How to be accurate in seizing
What has been caught by the eye
In an instant's flash—
Light through a petal,
Iridescence of clouds before sunrise.
They, too, are haunted by the need
To hold the fleeting still
In a design—
That vermilion under the haystack,
Struck at sunset,
Melting into the golden air
Yet perfectly defined,
An illuminated transience.

Today my house is lost in milk,
The milky veils of a blizzard.
The trees have turned pale.
There are no shadows,
That is the problem—no shadows
At all.

It is harder to see what one sees
Than anyone knows.
Monet knew, spent a lifetime
Trying to undazzle the light
And pin it down.

The flowers on my desk have been lit up one by one as by a spotlight as the sun slowly moves. And once more I am in a kind of ecstasy at the beauty of light through petals . . . how each vein is seen in relief, the structure suddenly visible.

These are the great days when clarity comes back to the air and all is a radiant suspense before the first leaf falls. Autumn is on the threshold, but for a week or two we have the best of everything. A still center before the wheel turns.

But the transcendent joy is the light now, the great autumn light at last. There is nothing like this light anywhere else in the world so far as I know—the great glory of New England. I have come back to my solitude, my joy, and I am sure these radiant skies have much to do with it.

And here in my study the sunlight is that autumn white, so clear, it calls for an inward act to match it . . . clarify, clarify.

Seeing it was like getting a transfusion of autumn light right to the vein.

Hour of Proof

It is the light, of course, and its great ways;
It comes like a celestial charity
With warmth not coldness in its clarity,
And through the violent green its violet rays
Anatomize each single leaf to shine,
The flesh transparent to the nerves' design.

A blade of grass, a frond of goldenrod,
A branch of beech paled to translucent green,
This is a world where structure counts again,
Flooded through by the presence of the god.
These simple days are coursed by a great cry,
A storm of radiance sweeping from the sky.

And when it comes a crimson petal up,
The lifeblood shows so brilliant in the vein,
A single flower dominates the green,
As if all earth were lifted in this cup,
And life began to flow the other way,
Up from the brimming petal to the sky . . .

As if the echoing rocks were to reflect,
And every open meadow to fulfill
The place and time where dancing growth is still,
And light and structure gently intersect;
Not the cold but the warmth of *caritas*
Shows us the summer green for what it was.

The autumn light X-rays our sealed-up riches;
We find within the milkweed a strange milk,
The folded seeds in parachutes of silk
That will fly soon to fall on fields and ditches.
Passionate summer's hour of proof is come:
Go we, my love, and catch a falling sun!

February Days

Who could tire of the long shadows,
The long shadows of the trees on snow?
Sometimes I stand at the kitchen window
For a timeless time in a long daze
Before these reflected perpendiculars,
Noting how the light has changed,
How tender it is now in February
When the shadows are blue not black.

The crimson cyclamen has opened wide,
A bower of petals drunk on the light,
And in the snow-bright ordered house
I am drowsy as a turtle in winter,
Living on light and shadow
And their changes.

Winter is the season when both animals and humans get stripped down to the marrow, but many animals hibernate, take the winter easy as it were; we humans are exposed naked to the currents of elation and depression. Here at Nelson it is the time of the most extraordinary light and the most perfect silence. When the first snow floats down on the rock-hard earth, first a flake at a time, then finally in soft white curtains, an entirely new silence falls. It feels as if one were being wound up into a cocoon, sealed in. There will be no escape, the primitive person senses, always with the same shiver of apprehension. At the same time, there is elation. One is lifted up in a cloud, a little above the earth, for soon there is no earth to be seen, only whiteness—whiteness without a shadow, while the snow falls. Is it dawn or dusk? Who can tell? And this goes on all night and occasionally all the next day, until there is no way out of the house. I am sealed in tight. Many times during the night I wake to listen, listen, but there is no sound at all. The silence is as thick and soft as wool. Will the snow ever stop falling?

But when at last the sun comes out again, we are born into a pristine world, into the snow light. The house has become a ship riding long white slopes of waves. The light!

The Snow Light

In the snow light,
In the swan light,
In the white-on-white light
Of a winter storm,
My delight and your delight
Kept each other warm.

The next afternoon
And love gone so soon!—
I met myself alone
In a windless calm,
Silenced at the bone
After the white storm.

What more was to come?
Out from the cocoon,
In the silent room,
Pouring out white light,
Amaryllis bloom
Opened in the night.

The cool petals shone
Like some winter moon
Or shadow of a swan,
Echoing the light
After you were gone
Of our white-on-white.

The Phoenix Again

On the ashes of this nest
Love wove with deathly fire
The phoenix takes its rest
Forgetting all desire.

After the flame, a pause,
After the pain, rebirth.
Obeying nature's laws
The phoenix goes to earth.

You cannot call it old
You cannot call it young.
No phoenix can be told,
This is the end of song.

It struggles now alone
Against death and self-doubt,
But underneath the bone
The wings are pushing out.

And one cold starry night
Whatever your belief
The phoenix will take flight
Over the seas of grief

To sing her thrilling song
To stars and waves and sky
For neither old nor young
The phoenix does not die.

Dutch Interior
Pieter de Hooch (1629-1682)

I recognize the quiet and the charm,
This safe enclosed room where a woman sews
And life is tempered, orderly, and calm.

Through the Dutch door, half-open, sunlight streams
And throws a pale square down on the red tiles.
The cozy black dog suns himself and dreams.

Even the bed is sheltered, it encloses,
A cupboard to keep people safe from harm,
Where copper glows with the warm flush of roses.

The atmosphere is all domestic, human,
Chaos subdued by the sheer power of need.
This is a room where I have lived as woman,

Lived too what the Dutch painter does not tell—
The wild skies overhead, dissolving, breaking,
And how that broken light is never still,

And how the roar of waves is always near,
What bitter tumult, treacherous and cold,
Attacks the solemn charm year after year!

It must be felt as peace won and maintained
Against those terrible antagonists—
How many from this quiet room have drowned?

How many left to go, drunk on the wind,
And take their ships into heartbreaking seas;
How many whom no woman's peace could bind?

Bent to her sewing, she looks drenched in calm.
Raw grief is disciplined to the fine thread.
But in her heart this woman is the storm;

Alive, deep in herself, holds wind and rain,
Remaking chaos into an intimate order
Where sometimes light flows through a windowpane.

Solitude

Loneliness is the poverty of self;
solitude is the richness of self.

At any moment solitude may put on the face of loneliness.

Solitude itself is a way of waiting for the inaudible and the invisible to make itself felt. And that is why solitude is never static and never hopeless.

How brief yet how full that first encounter between my new life and its first guests! So much greater, then, the sense of absence when the house and I found ourselves alone together after they had gone. It was my first experience of the transition back to solitude, the moment of loneliness, the shadowy moment before I can resume my real life here. The metaphor that comes to mind is that of a sea anemone that has been wide open to the tide, and then slowly closes up again as the tide ebbs. For alone here, I must first give up the world and all its dear, tantalizing human questions, first close myself away, and then, and only then, open to that other tide, the inner life, the life of solitude, which rises very slowly until, like the anemone, I am open to receive whatever it may bring.

Because I live alone and have for the past twenty years, I write from there. But I am becoming aware these days that of the two kinds of people who read me with the greatest interest—the first, people who live alone because they are widows, people to whom solitude has "happened," and the second, young people who have not yet made a commitment to life either in work or love—to the latter I may present a role model that is dangerous rather than helpful. I have come to represent the life of solitude as, per se, a valid choice as against marriage or even productive work. Maybe it is true that there are two times in life when solitude can be productive, when one is twenty and again after sixty. But of the two only in the former is solitude a choice. And in the former it is almost bound to be a temporary choice, for life is going to move in in all probability and change the course.

If one does choose solitude it must be for a purpose other than mere self-seeking; the search for "identity" is a fashionable concept these days, but sometimes at least it looks like pure self-indulgence. How does one find one's identity? My answer would be through work and through love, and both imply giving rather than getting. Each requires discipline, self-mastery, and a kind of selflessness, and they are each lifetime challenges. Who writes a perfect masterpiece or is a perfect lover?

There is no doubt that solitude is a challenge and to maintain balance within it a precarious business. But I must not forget that, for me, being with people or even with one beloved person for any length of time without solitude is even worse. I lose my center. I feel dispersed, scattered, in pieces. I must have time alone in which to mull over any encounter, and to extract its juice, its essence, to understand what has really happened to me as a consequence of it.

"Loneliness" for me is associated with love relationships. We are lonely when there is not perfect communion. In solitude one can achieve a good relationship with oneself.

Solitude has replaced the single intense relationship, the passionate love that even at Nelson focused all the rest. Solitude, like a long love, deepens with time, and, I trust, will not fail me if my own powers of creation diminish. For growing into solitude is one way of growing to the end.

I am here alone for the first time in weeks, to take up my "real" life again at last. That is what is strange—that friends, even passionate love, are not my real life unless there is time alone in which to explore and to discover what is happening or has happened. Without the interruptions, nourishing and maddening, this life would become arid. Yet I taste it fully only when I am alone here and "the house and I resume old conversations."

One of the facts about solitude is that one becomes as alert as an animal to every change of mood in the skies, and to every sound.

❧

Just how far and to what end would solitude take me? And how can one have the courage to shut life out when it knocks at the door?

❧

It occurs to me that boredom and panic are the two devils the solitary must combat. When I lay down this afternoon, I could not rest and finally got up because I was in a sweat of panic, panic for no definable reason, a panic of solitude, I presume.

❧

But there is something wrong when solitude such as mine can be "envied" by a happily married woman with children.

Mine is not, I feel sure, the best human solution. Nor have I ever thought it was. In my case it has perhaps made possible the creation of some works of art, but certainly it has done so at a high price in emotional maturity and in happiness. What I have is space around me and time around me. How they can be achieved in a marriage is the real question. It is not an easy one to answer.

Because I am well I no longer suffer from the acute loneliness I felt all spring and summer until now. Loneliness because in spite of all the kindnesses and concern of so many friends there was no one who could fill the hole at the center of my being—only myself could fill it by becoming whole again. It was loneliness for the *self*. Now that I can work, taking up the healthy rhythm of the days, I am not at all lonely.

❧

. . . I, in my normal life, am alone all the time. I work alone. Therefore, when someone comes for tea and it's the only person I see all day, that is precious too, because solitude without society would be meager and would, in the end, make for a dwindling of personality, perhaps. You can't eat yourself all day and all night. There has to be something coming in that brings life-food from the outside.

I was thinking about solitude, its supreme value. Here in Nelson I have been close to suicide more than once, and more than once have been close to a mystical experience of unity with the universe. The two states resemble each other: one has no wall, one is absolutely naked and diminished to essence. Then death would be the rejection of life because we cannot let go what we wish so hard to keep, but have to let go if we are to continue to grow.

When I talk about solitude I am really talking also about making space for that intense, hungry face at the window, starved cat, starved person. It is making space to *be there*. Lately a small tabby cat has come every day and stared at me with a strange, intense look. Of course I put food out, night and morning. She is so terrified that she runs away at once when I open the door, but she comes back to eat ravenously as soon as I disappear. Yet her hunger is clearly not only for food. I long to take her in my arms and hear her purr with relief at finding shelter. Will she ever become tame enough for that, to give in to what she longs to have? It is such an intense look with which she scans my face at the door before she runs away. It is not a pleading look, simply a huge question: "Can I trust?" Our two gazes hang on its taut thread. I find it painful.

Gestalt at Sixty

1

For ten years I have been rooted in these hills,
The changing light on landlocked lakes,
For ten years have called a mountain, friend,
Have been nourished by plants, still waters,
Trees in their seasons,
Have fought in this quiet place
For my *self*.

I can tell you that first winter
I heard the trees groan.
I heard the fierce lament
As if they were on the rack under the wind.
I too have groaned here,
Wept the wild winter tears.
I can tell you that solitude
Is not all exaltation, inner space
Where the soul breathes and work can be done.
Solitude exposes the nerve,
Raises up ghosts.
The past, never at rest, flows through it.

Who wakes in a house alone
Wakes to moments of panic.
(Will the roof fall in?
Shall I die today?)
Who wakes in a house alone
Wakes to inertia sometimes,
To fits of weeping for no reason.
Solitude swells the inner space
Like a balloon.
We are wafted hither and thither
On the air currents.
How to land it?

I worked out anguish in a garden.
Without the flowers,
The shadow of trees on snow, their punctuation,
I might not have survived.
I came here to create a world
As strong, renewable, fertile,
As the world of nature all around me—
Learned to clear myself as I have cleared the pasture,
Learned to wait,
Learned that change is always in the making
(Inner and outer) if one can be patient,
Learned to trust myself.

2

The house is receptacle of a hundred currents.
Letters pour in,
Rumor of the human ocean, never at rest,
Never still. . . .
Sometimes it deafens and numbs me.

I did not come here for society
In these years
When every meeting is collision,
The impact huge,
The reverberations slow to die down.
Yet what I have done here
I have not done alone,
Inhabited by a rich past of lives,
Inhabited also by the great dead,
By music, poetry—
Yeats, Valéry stalk through this house.
No day passes without a visitation—
Rilke, Mozart.
I am always a lover here,
Seized and shaken by love.

Lovers and friends,
I come to you starved
For all you have to give,
Nourished by the food of solitude,
A good instrument for all you have to tell me,
For all I have to tell you.
We talk of first and last things,
Listen to music together,
Climb the long hill to the cemetery
In autumn,
Take another road in spring
Toward newborn lambs.

No one comes to this house
Who is not changed.
I meet no one here who does not change me.

3

How rich and long the hours become,
How brief the years,
In this house of gathering,
This life about to enter its seventh decade.

I live like a baby
Who bursts into laughter
As a sunbeam on the wall,
Or like a very old woman
Entranced by the prick of stars
Through the leaves.

Just as the fruit gathers
All the riches of summer
Into its compact world,
I feel richer than ever before,
And breathe a larger air.

I am not ready to die,
But I am learning to trust death
As I have trusted life.
I am moving
Toward a new freedom
Born of detachment,
And a sweeter grace—
Learning to let go.

I am not ready to die,
But as I approach sixty
I turn my face toward the sea.
I shall go where tides replace time,
Where my world will open to a far horizon
Over the floating, never-still flux and change.
I shall go with the changes,
I shall look far out over golden grasses
And blue waters. . . .

There are no farewells.

Praise God for His mercies,
For His austere demands,
For His light
And for His darkness.

The Natural World

. . . if one looks long enough at almost anything, looks with absolute attention at a flower, a stone, the bark of a tree, grass, snow, a cloud, something like revelation takes place. Something is "given," and perhaps that something is always a reality *outside* the self. We are aware of God only when we cease to be aware of ourselves, not in the negative sense of denying the self, but in the sense of losing self in admiration and joy.

Whatever peace I know rests in the natural world, in feeling myself a part of it, even in a small way.

❧

For us who have no religion in the old-fashioned sense, who can say no prayers to a listening God, nature itself—nature and human love—polarize, and we pray by being fully aware of them both.

One thing is certain, and I have always known it—the joys of my life have nothing to do with age. They do not change. Flowers, the morning and evening light, music, poetry, silence, the goldfinches darting about . . .

What a thrill when the first skunk cabbage came out, thrusting its baroque green through moldy old leaves! I was starved for color as well as for motion in the static world, and that first bright green of the skunk cabbage was a tonic.

March-Mad

The strangely radiant skies have come
To lift us out of winter's gloom,
A paler more transparent blue,
A softer gold light on fresh snow.
It is a naked time that bares
Our slightly worn-down hopes and cares,
And sets us listening for frogs,
And sends us to seed catalogues
To bury our starved eyes and noses
In an extravagance of roses,
And order madly at this season
When we have had enough of reason.

Easter Morning

The extreme delicacy of this Easter morning
Spoke to me as a prayer and as a warning.
It was light on the brink, spring light
After a rain that gentled my dark night.
I walked through landscapes I had never seen
Where the fresh grass had just begun to green,
And its roots, watered deep, sprung to my tread;
The maples wore a cloud of feathery red,
But flowering trees still showed their clear design
Against the pale blue brightness chilled like wine.
And I was praying all the time I walked,
While starlings flew about, and talked, and talked.
Somewhere and everywhere life spoke the word.
The dead trees woke; each bush held its bird.
I prayed for delicate love and difficult,
That all be gentle now and know no fault,
That all be patient—as a wild rabbit fled
Sudden before me. Dear love, I would have said
(And to each bird who flew up from the wood),
I would be gentler still if that I could,
For on this Easter morning it would seem
The softest footfall danger is, extreme . . .
And so I prayed to be less than the grass
And yet to feel the Presence that might pass.
I made a prayer. I heard the answer, "Wait,
When all is so in peril, and so delicate!"

The maples, which had looked so old and forlorn all winter, were suddenly covered with small green umbrella-flowers. Shall I ever manage to be present in the hour they open? Always they have just arrived while my back was turned.

Metamorphosis

Always it happens when we are not there—
The tree leaps up alive into the air,
Small open parasols of Chinese green
Wave on each twig. But who has ever seen
The latch sprung, the bud as it burst?
Spring always manages to get there first.

Lovers of wind, who will have been aware
Of a faint stirring in the empty air,
Look up one day through a dissolving screen
To find no star, but this multiplied green,
Shadow on shadow, singing sweet and clear.
Listen, lovers of wind, the leaves are here!

Mozart Again

Now it is Mozart who comes back again
All garlanded in green.
Flute, harp, and trumpet, the sweet violin—
Each sound is seen.

Spring is a phrase, repeated green refrain,
Sound of new leaves springing.
I see the wind flowing like slanted rain,
Wind winging.

I learn this loving fresh, in ancient style
(Lightly time flows),
And mine a green world for pure joy awhile.
Listen, a rose!

Leaves are glissando. A long haunting phrase
Ripples the air—
This harpsichord of light that the wind plays.
Mozart is there.

When I am alone the flowers are really seen; I can pay attention to them. They are felt as presences. Without them I would die. Why do I say that? Partly because they change before my eyes. They live and die in a few days; they keep me closely in touch with process, with growth, and also with dying. I am floated on their moments.

A Flower-Arranging Summer

The white walls of this airy house assume
Flowers as natural and needed friends;
All summer long while flowers are in bloom
Attentive expectation never ends.
The day begins with walking through wet grass
In a slow progress, to visit the whole garden,
And all is undecided as I pass,
For here I must be thief and also warden:
What must I leave? What can I bear to plunder?
What fragile freshness, what amazing throat
Has opened in the night, what single wonder
That will be sounded like a single note,
When these light wandering thoughts deploy
Before the grave deeds of decisive joy?

Later, I cut judiciously and fill my basket.
It's a fine clamor of unrelated voices,
As I begin the day's adventure and slow task,
The delicate, absorbing task of choices—
That lavender and pink that need some acid,
Perhaps a saffron zinnia, linen-crisp?
Or poppy's crinkle beside the rich and placid
Rose petal, and some erratic plume or wisp
To enhance cosmos, its flat symmetry,
And always the poised starry phlox in masses—
Sometimes I have undone the same bouquet
A dozen times in six different glasses,
A dozen times and still dissatisfied,
As if that day my wish had been denied.

Sometimes two poppies can compose a world,
Two and one seed-pagoda on a hairy stem,
Blood-red, vermilion, each entity unfurled
Clashes its cymbals in the silent room;
The scale so small, substance diaphanous,
Yet the reverberation of that twofold red
Has focused one room for me ever since,
As if an Absolute had once been said.
Sometimes the entire morning does get lost
In ochers, greenish-whites, in warm deep rose,
As I pick all the zinnias against frost,
Salmon, crude red, magenta—and who knows
What harsh loud chords of music sweep the room?
Both chords and discords, till the whole bright thing
Explodes into a brilliant cloud of bloom,
And the white walls themselves begin to sing.

And so the morning's gone, Was this to waste it
In a long foolish flowery meditation?
Time slides away, and how are we to taste it?
Within the floating world all is sensation.
And yet I see eternity's long wink
In these elusive games, and only there:
When I can so suspend myself to think,
I seem suspended in undying air.

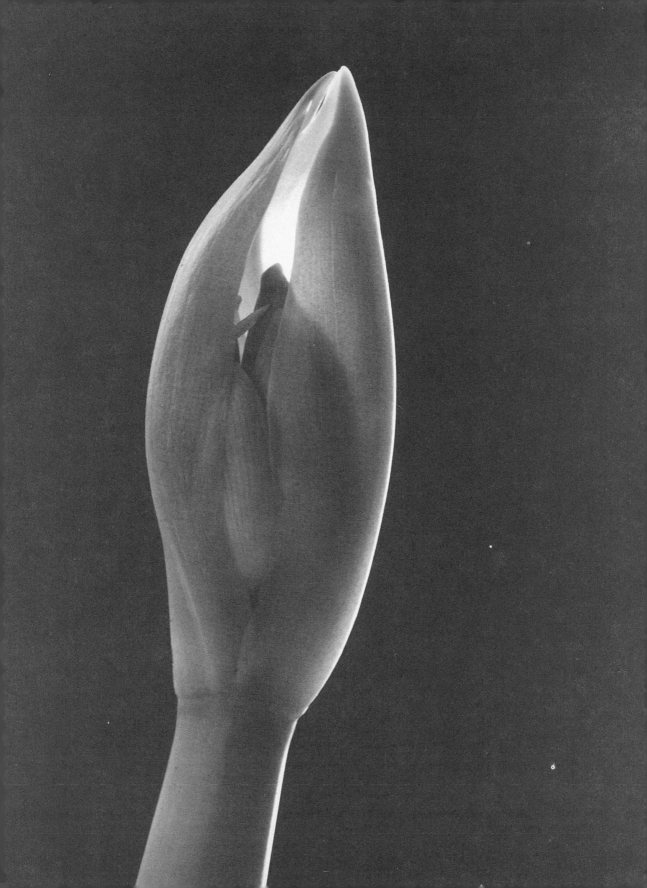

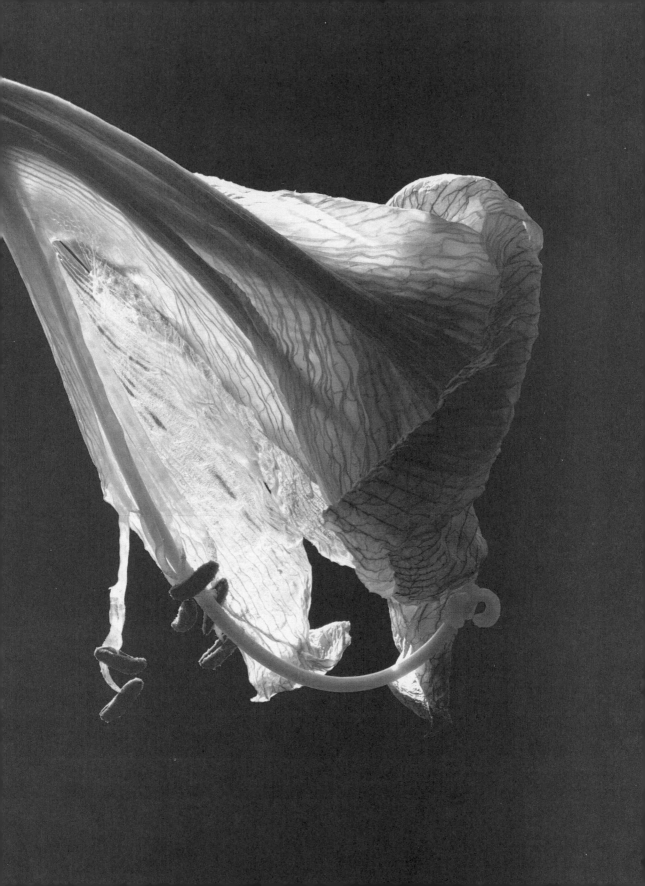

For the joys a garden brings are already going as they come. They are poignant. When the first apple falls with that tremendous thud, one of the big seasonal changes startles the heart. The swanlike peony suddenly lets all its petals fall in a snowy pile, and it is time to say good-by until another June. But by then the delphinium is on the way, and the lilies . . . the flowers ring their changes through a long cycle, a cycle that will be renewed. That is what the gardener often forgets. To the flowers we never have to say good-by forever. *We* grow older every year, but not the garden; it is reborn every spring.

❧

There the door is always open into the "holy"—growth, birth, death. Every flower holds the whole mystery in its short cycle, and in the garden we are never far away from death, the fertilizing, good, *creative* death.

❧

When I am gardening I do not think of anything at all; I am wholly involved in the physical work and when I go in, I feel whole again, centered. Why? I think maybe it is because when things pile up one does nothing with the whole of oneself. The next thing on the calendar is already moving in before one has finished whatever it is one is at. Then pressure builds up. Gardening empties the mind.

It is a mellow day, very gentle. The ash has lost its leaves and when I went out to get the mail and stopped to look up at it, I rejoiced to think that soon everything here will be honed down to structure. It is all a rich farewell now to leaves, to color. I think of the trees and how simply they let go, let fall the riches of a season, how without grief (it seems) they can let go and go deep into their roots for renewal and sleep. . . .

Does anything in nature despair except man? An animal with a foot caught in a trap does not seem to despair. It is too busy trying to survive. It is all closed in, to a kind of still, intense waiting. Is this a key? Keep busy with survival. Imitate the trees. Learn to lose in order to recover, and remember that nothing stays the same for long, not even pain, psychic pain. Sit it out. Let it all pass. Let it go.

All the way down I had been in a state of great praise for trees wondering . . . how I could ever live without them, thinking of their comfort, how they nourish and sustain us with their beauty and coolness, their steadfastness, the fact that they will outlive those who plant them. And I understood why old men plant trees.

All Day I Was with Trees

Across wild country on solitary roads
Within a fugue of parting, I was consoled
By birches' sovereign whiteness in sad woods,
Dark glow of pines, a single elm's distinction—
I was consoled by trees.

In February we see the structure change—
Or the light change, and so the way we see it.
Tensile and delicate, the trees stand now
Against the early skies, the frail fresh blue,
In an attentive stillness.

Naked, the trees are singularly present,
Although their secret force is still locked in.
Who could believe that the new sap is rising
And soon we shall draw up amazing sweetness
From stark maples?

All day I was with trees, a fugue of parting,
All day lived in long cycles, not brief hours.
A tenderness of light before new falls of snow
Lay on the barren landscape like a promise.
Love nourished every vein.

Leaves before the Wind

We have walked, looking at the actual trees:
The chestnut leaves wide-open like a hand,
The beech leaves bronzing under every breeze,
We have felt flowing through our knees
        As if we were the wind.

We have sat silent when two horses came,
Jangling their harness, to mow the long grass.
We have sat long and never found a name
For this suspension in the heart of flame
        That does not pass.

We have said nothing; we have parted often,
Not looking back, as if departure took
An absolute of will—once not again
(But this is each day's feat, as when
        The heart first shook).

Where fervor opens every instant so,
There is no instant that is not a curve,
And we are always coming as we go;
We lean toward the meeting that will show
        Love's very nerve.

And so exposed (O leaves before the wind!)
We bear this flowing fire, forever free,
And learn through devious paths to find
The whole, the center, and perhaps unbind
        The mystery

Where there are no roots, only fervent leaves,
Nourished on meditations and the air,
Where all that comes is also all that leaves,
And every hope compassionately lives
        Close to despair.

Problems to do with climate, with snow or drought or high wind, problems to do with growing things, bring one right down to the marrow. They quickly become metaphor in the mind; they are the stuff of poetry.

The storm has come, with wild white veils, high wind. I can't see the ocean . . . really it is thrilling to be so isolated in such a fierce white wilderness of a world.

At last I look out on an ermine field! The whole landscape has become rich and strange since the snow last night. The harsh ice has given way to this opulent softness and we can celebrate the festival of winter . . .

How beautiful the white field is in its blur of falling snow, with the delicate black pencil strokes of trees and bushes seen through it! And, of course, the silence, the snow silence, becomes hypnotic if one stops to listen.

Snow Fall

With no wind blowing
It sifts gently down,
Enclosing my world in
A cool white down,
A tenderness of snowing.

It falls and falls like sleep
Till wakeful eyes can close
On all the waste and loss
As peace comes in and flows,
Snow-dreaming what I keep.

Silence assumes the air
And the five senses all
Are wafted on the fall
To somewhere magical
Beyond hope and despair.

There is nothing to do
But drift now, more or less
On some great lovingness,
On something that does bless,
The silent, tender snow.

Twelve Below

A bitter gale
Over frozen snow
Burns the skin like hail.
It is twelve below.

Too cold to live
Too cold to die
Warm animals wait
And make no cry.

Their feathers puff
Their eyes are bright
Their fur expands.
Warm animals wait.

They make no sign
They waste no breath
In this cold country
Between life and death.

What is it about animals? Joanna wondered as she stroked the soft nose of Ulysses and looked into his deep brown eye, so tender and yet so remote. Is it that animals rest and nourish some deep natural being in us; they make us young and merry again; they restore us to childhood's world, pure and self-absorbed . . . and they do this partly because the means of communication are so very simple, a meal, a caress . . .

Small Joys
New Year 1990

What memory keeps fresh, frames unspoken,
I catch for you, innumerable friends.
When so much else has been destroyed or broken
These joys remain intact as the year ends,
A year of earth-grief and of bitter news,
The starving children and the burning trees,
Otters coated in oil and dolphins drowned.
Small joys keep life alive. I give you these.
They will not die, you know. They are around.

When the long winter lingered on
And all the color stayed an ugly brown,
Suddenly snowdrops had pushed their way through
And their sharp whiteness made all new.

Early in February owls began to woo,
Their language gentle, calling "Who? Who? Who?"
And I was lit up when an awesome bird
In the harsh cold spoke such a tender word.

The finches changed their suits early this year
From olive to bright gold, and there they were
Burbling as always, their busy flight a whir
Of yellow weaving through the static air.

The daffodils in April thronged the grass
And all along the wood's edge, fabulous
To show the thousand faces of a nation,
Expected, still beyond all expectation.

Later in June, alive with silent fire,
The fireflies pulsed their firefly desire
And from the terrace I could watch the dance,
Follow their bliss. It happened only once.

Full summer brought nasturtiums in profusion
I picked and bent to drink the sweet confusion,
Yellow and orange, the fresh scent. I could
Keep summer in a bowl for days, and did.

One autumn night my cat ran to my call
And leapt five feet over the terrace wall.
A second, weightless, he flowed and did not fall,
That silver splendor, princely and casual.

And last I give you murmur of waves breaking,
The sound of sleep that is a kind of waking
As the tide rises from the distant ocean
And all is still and yet all in motion.

The small joys last and even outlast earthquake.
I give you these for love—and for hope's sake.

Love

When I said that all poems are love poems, I meant that the motor power, the electric current is love of one kind or another. The subject may be something quite impersonal . . .

Invocation

Come out of the dark earth
Here where the minerals
Glow in their stone cells
Deeper than seed or birth.

Come under the strong wave
Here where the tug goes
As the tide turns and flow
Below that architrave.

Come into the pure air
Above all heaviness
Of storm and cloud to this
Light-possessed atmosphere.

Come into, out of, under
The earth, the wave, the air.
Love, touch us everywhere
With primeval candor.

Dream

Inside my mother's death
I lay and could not breathe,
Under the hollow cheekbone,
Under the masked face,
As if locked under stone
In that terrible place.

I knew before I woke
That I would have to break
Myself out of that tomb,
Be born again or die,
Once more wrench from the womb
The prisoner's harsh cry.

And that the only way
Was to bring death with me
From under the lost face,
For I would never come
From that empty place
Without her, alone:

Her death within me
Like the roots of a tree,
Her life within mine—
Twice-born mystery
Where the roots intertwine.
When I woke, I was free.

Because passionate love breaks down walls and at first does it in such a sovereign way, we are rarely willing to admit how little that initial barrier-breaking is going to count when it comes to the slow, difficult, accepting of each other, when it comes to the irritations and abrasions, and the collisions, too, between two isolated human beings who want to be joined in a lasting relationship. So the walls go up again. The moment's vision is clouded, and mostly, I believe, by the fear of pain, our own and that of the other's, by the fear of rejection. To be honest is to expose wounds, and also to wound. There is no preventing that. Union on a deep level is so costly that it very rarely takes place. But withdrawal, censorship, the wish to keep the surfaces smooth because any eruption spells danger and must therefore be prevented, is costly also. Censorship simply drives conflict deeper inside. What is never discussed does not for that reason cease to exist. On the contrary, it may fester and finally become a killing poison.

A Light Left On

In the evening we came back
Into our yellow room,
For a moment taken aback
To find the light left on,
Falling on silent flowers,
Table, book, empty chair
While we had gone elsewhere,
Had been away for hours.

When we came home together
We found the inside weather.
All of our love unended
The quiet light demanded,
And we gave, in a look
At yellow walls and open book.
The deepest world we share
And do not talk about
But have to have, was there,
And by that light found out.

Mourning to Do

The new year and a fresh fall of snow,
The new year and mourning to do
Alone here in the lovely silent house,
Alone as the inner eye opens at last—
Not as the shutter of a camera with a click,
But like a gentle waking in a dark room
Before dawn when familiar objects take on
Substance out of their shadowy corners
And come to life. So with my lost love,
For years lost in the darkness of her mind,
Tied to a wheelchair, not knowing where she was
Or who she had been when we lived together
In amity, peaceful as turtle doves.

Judy is dead. Judy is gone forever.

I cannot fathom that darkness, nor know
Whether the true spirit is alive again.
But what I do know is the peace of it,
And in the darkened room before dawn, I lie
Awake and let the good tears flow at last,
And as light touches the chest of drawers
And the windows grow transparent, rest,
Happy to be mourning what was singular
And comforting as the paintings on the wall,
All that can now come to life in my mind,
Good memories fresh and sweet as the dawn—
Judy drinking her tea with a cat on her lap,
And our many little walks before suppertime.
So it is now the gentle waking to what was,
And what is and will be as long as I am alive.
"Happy grieving," someone said who knew—
Happy the dawn of memory and the sunrise.

My chief reason for Thanksgiving is, of course, my friends. From there I went to looking around the room and celebrating a few of them. There is a constant flow of love coming toward me like a daily tide which lifts me up after the difficulties of the morning, always hard these days because of cramps. I begin by midmorning to emerge into the kindly light of love.

I can cast out the wrong idea of fidelity and understand that in the end one cannot be faithful in the true life-giving sense if it means being unfaithful to oneself.

The Ballad of Johnny
(*A News Item*)

For safety on the expedition
A name-tag on each child was hung.
A necklace-name, his very own,
So he could not get lost for long.

Johnny jumped up and down for joy
To have a name forever true.
"I'm Johnny," cried the little boy.
"Johnny is going to the zoo!"

"Johnny," he whispered in the subway.
His whole face was suffused with bliss.
This was the best, the greatest day.
Boldly he gave his name a kiss.

But soon forgot it at the zoo
And let the name-tag swing out free,
For could that elephant be true?
And there was so much there to see . . .

Look, Johnny, at the monkey swinging
High in the air on his trapeze!
He heard the gibbon's sharp shrill singing
And begged to hold the monkey, please.

Then saw a goat and ran off fast
To hug the dear fantastic thing,
An animal to stroke at last,
A living toy for all his loving.

The soft lips nibbled at his sweater
And Johnny laughed with joy to feel
Such new-found friendliness and, better,
To know this animal was real.

His face was breathing in fur coat,
He did not notice anything
As gentle lips and greedy throat
Swallowed the name-tag and the string.

But when he found that they were gone
And he had lost his name for good,
Dreadful it was to be alone,
And Johnny screamed his terror loud.

The friendly goat was strange and wild,
And the cold eyes' indifferent stare
Could give no comfort to the child
Who had become No one, Nowhere.

"I've lost my name. I'm going to die,"
He shouted when his teacher came
And found him too afraid to cry.
"But, Johnny, you still have your name!

"It's not a tag, it's in your head,
And you are Johnny through and through.
Look in the mirror," teacher said,
"There's Johnny looking out at you."

But he had never had a mirror,
And Johnny met there a strange child
And screamed dismay at this worse error,
And only grew more lost and wild.

"No, no," he screamed, "that is not me,
That ugly boy I don't know who . . ."
Great treasure lost, identity,
When a goat ate it at the zoo.

We have to keep the channels in ourselves open to pain. At the same time it is essential that true joys be experienced, that the sunrise not leave us unmoved, for civilization depends on the true joys, all those that have nothing to do with money or affluence—nature, the arts, human love.

❧

Life must flow through you at every moment and every day and through every year. You're really a receptacle, an instrument for life to flow through and if you keep stopping it by over control, it's not good. It's not good I mean whether you're a creator or not.

❧

I've tried to be honest. It's harder than it looks in a book that you know is going to be published to find the right line between indiscretion or between sort of self-exposure in the negative sense *and* to try to give, to be open, to be absolutely open and transparent. Again, the word "transparent" which is very dear to me. I try to be transparent in my human relations and in my work. But, of course, that makes you very vulnerable and few people dare. It's too dangerous.

The more our bodies fail us, the more naked and more demanding is the spirit, the more open and loving we can become if we are not afraid of what we are and of what we feel.

✹

One of the censors that has been at work has been the notion that to be in love at our age is ludicrous and somehow not proper, that passionate love can be banished after sixty shall we say? That is one of the myths that has been around a long time, but it was never true. Love at any age has its preposterous side—that is why it comes as a kind of miracle at any age. It is never commonplace, never to be experienced without a tremor. But to stop arbitrarily the flow of life because of a preconceived idea, any preconceived idea, is to damage the truth of the inner person . . . that is dangerous. Are we not on earth to love each other? And to grow? And how does one grow except through love, except through opening ourselves to other human beings to be fertilized and made new?

Of Molluscs

As the tide rises, the closed mollusc
Opens a fraction to the ocean's food,
Bathed in its riches. Do not ask
What force would do, or if force could.

A knife is of no use against a fortress.
You might break it to pieces as gulls do.
No, only the rising tide and its slow progress
Opens the shell. Lovers, I tell you true.

You who have held yourselves closed hard
Against warm sun and wind, shelled up in fears
And hostile to a touch or tender word—
The ocean rises, salt as unshed tears.

Now you are floated on this gentle flood
That cannot force or be forced, welcome food
Salt as your tears, the rich ocean's blood,
Eat, rest, be nourished on the tide of love.

The Great Transparencies

Lately I have been thinking much of those,
The open ones, the great transparencies,
Through whom life—is it wind or water?—flows
Unstinted, who have learned the sovereign ease.
They are not young; they are not ever young.

Youth is too vulnerable to bear the tide,
And let it rise, and never hold it back,
Then let it ebb, not suffering from pride,
Nor thinking it must ebb from private lack.
The elders yield because they are so strong—

Seized by the great wind like a ripening field,
All rippled over in a sensuous sweep,
Wave after wave, lifted and glad to yield,
But whether wind or water, never keep
The tide from flowing or hold it back for long.

Lately I have been thinking much of these,
The unafraid although still vulnerable,
Through whom life flows, the great transparencies,
The old and open, brave and beautiful . . .
They are not young; they are not ever young.

Time

Childhood is a place as well as a time.

Spring is always poignant because nothing stays. It must be caught and appreciated on the wing, for soon it will be gone.

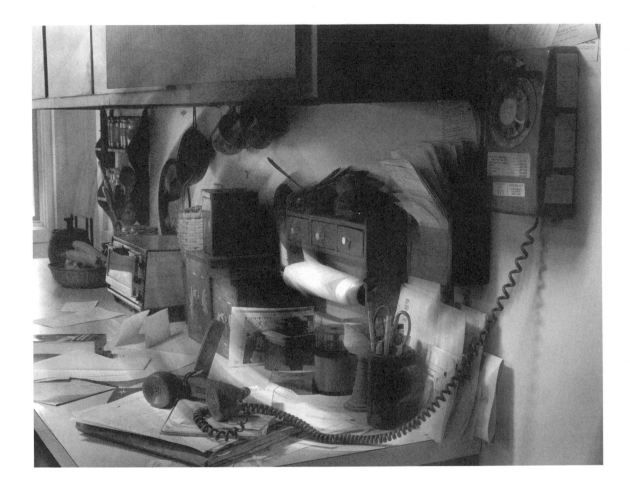

As far as I can see from here almost everyone I know is trying to do the impossible every day. All mothers, all writers, all artists of every kind, every human being who has work to do and still wants to stay human and to be responsive to another human beings' needs, joys, and sorrows. There is never enough time and that's the rub. In my case every choice I make means depriving someone. I write one letter and have to push another aside. I go away for a few days to see a friend, and lose the thread of the journal. . . . I live in a perpetual state of guilt about the "undone." Probably everyone does?

❦

I feel cluttered when there is no time to analyze experience. That is the silt— unexplored experience that literally chokes the mind. Too much comes into this house—books I am asked to read and comment on, manuscripts, letters, an old friend who wants my opinion about a journal (whether it is publishable), and so on. *This* is the clutter, not woodchuck or raccoon!

❦

It is harder for women, perhaps, to be "one-pointed," much harder for them to clear space around whatever it is they want to do beyond household chores and family life. Their lives are fragmented . . . this is the cry I get in so many letters— the cry not so much for "a room of one's own" as time of one's own. Conflict becomes acute, whatever it may be about, when there is no margin left on any day in which to try at least to resolve it.

❦

Being "active," "doing something" may be an escape from loafing for when one loafs the imagination springs into being and all kinds of unexpected things may happen in the psyche. Compulsive "doers" are at least sometimes deliberately escaping themselves, or their *selves*.

The crisis of middle age has to do as much as anything with a catastrophic anxiety about time itself. How has one managed to come to the meridian and still be so far from the real achievement one had dreamed possible at twenty? And I mean achievement as a human being as well as within a career.

I have time to think. That is the great, the greatest luxury. I have time to be. Therefore my responsibility is huge. To use time well and to be all that I can in whatever years are left to me. This does not dismay.

It is worth everything to me to feel the morning opening gently, not to be hurried, not to push myself from one kind of response to another at top speed.

※

Today I feel centered and time is a friend instead of the old enemy. It was zero this morning. I have a fire burning in my study, yellow roses and mimosa on my desk. There is an atmosphere of festival, of release, in the house. We are one, the house and I, and I am happy to be alone—time to think, time to be. This kind of open-ended time is the only luxury that really counts and I feel stupendously rich to have it.

※

My hope that I would have a whole series of empty days, days without interruption, days in which to think and laze, (for creation depends as much on laziness as on hard work), was, of course, impossible.

※

I reach and have reached the timeless moment, the pure suspension within time, only through love. . . .

So what I said the day before yesterday about the timeless moment being associated for me only with passionate love was not quite true. Maybe the timeless moment comes to us when we are centered and so can truly *see*.

I knew, from having watched my father hack down the incredible amount of work he accomplished day by day and year by year, how supportive a routine is, how the spirit moves around freely in it as it does in a plain New England church. Routine is not a prison, but the way into freedom from time. The apparently measured time has immeasurable space within it, and in this it resembles music.

These Images Remain [an excerpt]

These images remain, these classic landscapes
That lie, immense and quiet, behind eyes
Enlarged by love to think only in shapes
That compass time and frame the changing skies,
Triumph of arch, of spire, triumph of trees,
The pure perspective, the poignant formal scene.
Pursued by time, still we were given these;
Even the flames of spring seemed frozen green,
Fountains suspended crystal on the air,
And every open square could make us glad.
Where we stood once, once free to stand and stare,
Imagination wanders like a god.
These images exist. They have not changed,
Though we are caught by time, by time estranged.

On Being Given Time

Sometimes it seems to be the inmost land
All children still inhabit when alone.
They play the game of morning without end,
And only lunch can bring them, startled, home
Bearing in triumph a small speckled stone.

Yet even for them, too much dispersal scatters;
What complex form the simplest game may hold!
And all we know of time that really matters
We've learned from moving clouds and waters
Where we see form and motion lightly meld.

Not the clock's tick and its relentless bind
But the long ripple that opens out beyond
The duck as he swims down the tranquil pond,
Or when a wandering, falling leaf may find
And follow the formal downpath of the wind.

It is, perhaps, our most complex creation,
A lovely skill we spend a lifetime learning,
Something between the world of pure sensation
And the world of pure thought, a new relation,
As if we held in balance the globe turning.

Even a year's not long, yet moments are.
This moment, yours and mine, and always given,
When the leaf falls, the ripple opens far,
And we go where all animals and children are,
The world is open. Love can breathe again.

Creation Itself

If you are a writer or an artist, it is work that fulfills and makes you come into wholeness, and that goes on through a lifetime. Whatever the wounds that have to heal, the moment of creation assures that all is well, that one is still in tune with the universe, that the inner chaos can be probed and distilled into order and beauty.

Prayer before Work

Great one, austere,
By whose intent the distant star
Holds its course clear,
Now makes this spirit soar—
Give it that ease.

Out of the absolute
Abstracted grief, comfortless, mute,
Sound the clear note,
Pure, piercing as the flute:
Give it precision.

Austere, great one,
By whose grace the inalterable song
May still be wrested from
The corrupt lung:
Give it strict form.

Girl with 'Cello

There had been no such music here until
A girl came in from falling dark and snow
To bring into this house her glowing 'cello
As if some silent, magic animal.

She sat, head bent, her long hair all aspill
Over the breathing wood, and drew the bow.
There had been no such music here until
A girl came in from falling dark and snow.

And she drew out that sound so like a wail,
A rich dark suffering joy, as if to show
All that a wrist holds and that fingers know
When they caress a magic animal.
There had been no such music here until
A girl came in from falling dark and snow.

. . . every artist is androgynous, that it is the masculine in a woman and the feminine in a man that proves creative. This I have always believed.

※

. . . the woman who needs to create works of art is born with a kind of psychic tension in her which drives her unmercifully to find a way to balance, to make herself whole. Every human being has this need: in the artist it is mandatory. Unable to fulfill it, he goes mad. But when the artist is a woman she fulfills it at the *expense* of herself as a woman.

※

How can I be sure that all the years I have sat at a desk add up to anything worth having, as against what I might have done had I, for instance, devoted myself to teaching underprivileged children? This is the demon of guilt who points out that what Colette calls a life of self-torture may in fact be the purest self-indulgence.

It is only when we can believe that we are creating the soul that life has any meaning, but when we can believe it—and I do and always have—then there is nothing we do that is without meaning and nothing that we suffer that does not hold the seed of creation in it.

I would like to believe when I die that I have given myself away like a tree that sows seeds every spring and never counts the loss, because it is not loss, it is adding to future life. It is the tree's way of being. Strongly rooted perhaps, but spilling out its treasure on the wind.

I am, I think, more of a poet than I was before I knew him, if to be a poet means allowing life to flow through one rather than forcing it to a mold the will has shaped; if it means learning to let the day shape the work, not the work, the day, and so live toward essence as naturally as a bird or a flower.

A Recognition
For Perley Cole

I wouldn't know how rare they come these days,
But I know Perley's rare. I know enough
To stop fooling around with words, and praise
This man who swings a scythe in subtle ways,
And brings green order, carved out of the rough.
I wouldn't know how rare, but I discover
They used to tell an awkward learning boy,
"Keep the heel down, son, careful of the swing!"
I guess at perils and peril makes me sing.
So let the world go, but hold fast to joy,
And praise the craftsman till Hell freezes over!

I watched him that first morning when the dew
Still slightly bent tall, toughened grasses,
Sat up in bed to watch him coming through
Holding the scythe so lightly and so true
In slow sweeps and in lovely passes,
The swing far out, far out—but not too far,
The pause to wipe and whet the shining blade.
I felt affinities: farmer and poet
Share a good deal, although they may not know it.
It looked as easy as when the world was made,
And God could pull a bird out or a star.

For there was Perley in his own sweet way
Pulling some order out of ragged land,
Cutting the tough, chaotic growth away,
So peace could saunter down a summer day,
For here comes Cole with genius in his hand!
I saw in him a likeness to that flame,
Brancusi, in his Paris studio,
Who pruned down, lifted from chaotic night
Those naked, shining images of flight—
The old man's gentle malice and bravado,
Boasting hard times: It was my game!"

"*C'était mon jeu!*"—to wrest joy out of pain,
The endless skillful struggle to uncloud
The clouded vision, to reduce and prune,
And bring back from the furnace, fired again,
A world of magic, joy alone allowed.
Now Perley says, "God damn it!"—and much worse.
Hearing him, I get back some reverence.
Could you, they ask, call such a man your friend?
Yes (damn it!), and yes world without end!
Brancusi's game and his make the same sense,
And not unlike a prayer is Perley's curse.

So let the rest go, and heel down, my boy,
And praise the artist till Hell freezes over,
For he is rare, he with his scythe (no toy),
He with his perils, with his skill and joy,
Who comes to prune, to make clear, to uncover,
The old man, full of wisdom, in his prime.
There in the field, watching him as he passes,
I recognize that violent, gentle blood,
Impatient patience. I would, if I could,
Call him my kin, there scything down the grasses,
Call him my good luck in a dirty time.

What kept me going was, I think, that writing for me is a way of understanding what is happening to me, of thinking hard things out. I have never written a book that was not born out of a question I needed to answer for myself. Perhaps it is the need to remake order out of chaos over and over again. For art is order, but it is made out of the chaos of life.

❦

When I am really inspired I can put a poem through a hundred drafts and keep my excitement. But this sustained battle is possible only when I am in a state of grace, when the deep channels are open, and when they are, when I am both profoundly stirred and balanced, then poetry comes as a gift from powers beyond my will.

❦

As I look back, now, on the whole sequence of that bad time, I have no regrets. We have to make myths of our lives; it is the only way to live them without despair. This is not to dramatize so much as to look for and come to understand the metaphor that reality always holds in it. The inner world, the world of poetry, is as much nourished by the bad times as by anything.

Eine Kleine Snailmusik

"The snail watchers are interested in snails from all angles. . . . At the moment they are investigating the snail's reactions to music. 'We have played to them on the harp in the garden and in the country on the pipe,' said Mr. Heaton, 'and we have taken them into the house and played to them on the piano.'"

—*The London Star*

What soothes the angry snail?
What's music to his horn?
For the "Sonata Appassionata,"
He shows scorn,
And Handel
Makes the frail snail
Quail,
While Prokofieff
Gets no laugh,
And Tchaikovsky, I fear,
No tear.
Piano, pipe, and harp,
Dulcet or shrill,
Flat or sharp,
Indoors or in the garden,
Are willy-nilly
Silly
To the reserved, slow,
Sensitive
Snail,
Who prefers to live
Glissandissimo,
Pianissimo.

Journey toward Poetry

First that beautiful mad exploration
Through a multiple legend of landscape
When all roads open and then close again
Behind a car that rushes toward escape,
The mind shot out across foreign borders
To visionary and abrupt disorders.
The hills unwind and wind up on a spool;
Rivers leap out of their beds and run;
The pink geranium standing on the wall
Rests there a second, still, and then breaks open
To show far off the huge blood-red cathedral
Looming like magic against a bright blue sky;
And marble graveyards fall into the sea.

After the mad beautiful racing is done,
To be still, to be silent, to stand by a window
Where time not motion changes light to shadow,
Is to be present at the birth of creation.
Now from the falling chaos of sensation
A single image possesses the whole soul:
The field of wheat, the telegraph pole.
From them the composed imagination reaches
Up and down to find its own frontier.
All landscapes crystallize and focus here—
And in the distance stand five copper beeches.

Afterword

My work on *From May Sarton's Well* has been a very personal project from the beginning, before the idea of a book even became a dream. In the Preface I spoke of May's influence on me as a person and a photographer. Her interest and support helped this book become a reality. As my work on this project developed, May's encouragement and advice has become more direct. I want to close here with a few reflections on the woman I have come to feel is a friend.

I have never known anyone more passionate about life, more dedicated to her work, or more giving of herself to her friends. I first experienced her passion relating to her work the second time I saw her in person. I attended a book-signing reception for May in Hartford, Connecticut, in 1980, celebrating the publication of *Recovering* and *Halfway to Silence*. As I approached the table where she was autographing books, someone asked a question concerning reviews of her work. I found myself standing in front of May Sarton, her eyes directed at me, as she nearly exploded with anger over the lack of notice she had received from the influential critics. Over the years, I have come to understand how the energy in her anger helps fuel her creative output, even though that anger can be hard for a recipient to handle.

About the time of the book-signing, my friend Anne Alvord and I gave our first talk on Sarton. Over the next few years, we corresponded with May concerning the various programs we were presenting about her work. Whether handwritten or typed, May's letters evidenced her mind's fast pace. I suspect that her tiny handwriting often takes longer for recipients to decipher than for her to write.

One handwritten note from May was an invitation to visit her at "Wild Knoll"—her home in York, Maine—and show her my photographs that I was organizing into an exhibition to be titled "Photographic Reflections on Words by May Sarton." On a July morning in 1983, Anne and I found ourselves, nervous as school children, following complicated directions to her home, a place we felt was already familiar after reading *The House by the Sea*.

May's home is an eloquent poem about the woman who lives and works there. Sun pours through the windows and plays a song of light and shadow as the day progresses. The natural world of her garden—an extensive field leading gently to the sea, birds and squirrels at her feeders—is always visible through the large windows, and flowers are beautifully arranged inside. The love of friends is felt through stuffed animals here and there—apparently gifts from those who know her well—and the photographs of people on her desks. Her typewriter, cluttered writing desk, books shelved and in piles for constant access, art objects—all speak of her own creativity and her appreciation of the creativity of others. The spaciousness of her house and the land, and the presence of the tidal sea, give a sense of the rhythm and space of time. Only two houses are visible from her home, and they are beyond shouting distance. Wild Knoll is a place where a unique woman works and lives alone, where solitude enables her to write, but where it is also often lonely, especially these years when she is plagued with ill health.

The routine of caring for herself and her cat, feeding the wild birds and squirrels, tending the garden and the house—all that used to sustain May—now sometimes becomes an insurmountable burden. Still she retains her sense of humor. She may tell a caller about the difficulties she is having, her pain and frustrations, but with whatever energy she has left, she finds something to laugh about, a rich laugh releasing all tension.

I mentioned May's generosity to her friends, how much she gives of herself. I have experienced that generosity both through her work and personally, with her encouragement for and support of my project, even when she had doubts about illustrating poetry with the visual art of photography. May taught me that poems are interpreted differently by each individual and should be presented on their own; photographs are appropriate accompaniment for prose. She also guided me through the process of obtaining the rights to use her copyrighted work at a reasonable price.

I am concluding this book with an abridged album of May and her home at Wild Knoll, and I express my eternal gratitude to her.

References

p. 1   *As Does New Hampshire and Other Poems* (Richard R. Smith Publishers, 1967), p. 37; and *Collected Poems: 1930–1993* (W. W. Norton and Company, 1974), p. 313.

p. 2   *Journal of a Solitude* (W. W. Norton & Company, Inc., 1973), p. 48.

p. 5   *Letters from Maine: New Poems* (W. W. Norton and Company, 1984), p. 37; and *Collected Poems: 1930–1993*, p. 474.

p. 6   *The House by the Sea: A Journal* (W. W. Norton and Company, 1977), p. 61.

p. 8   *Recovering: A Journal 1978–1979* (W. W. Norton and Company, 1980), p. 185.

p. 10   *Journal of a Solitude*, p. 48.

p. 10   Ibid, p. 33.

p. 10   Ibid, p. 35.

p. 12   *Cloud, Stone, Sun, Vine: Poems, Selected and New* (W. W. Norton & Company, 1961), p. 142; and *Collected Poems: 1930–1993*, p. 223.

p. 13   *A Durable Fire:* New Poems (W. W. Norton and Company, 1972), p. 51; and *Collected Poems: 1930–1993*, p. 390.

p. 15   *Plant Dreaming Deep* (W. W. Norton and Company, 1968), pp. 85–86.

p. 16   *Selected Poems of May Sarton*, Edited and with an Introduction by Serena Sue Hilsinger and Lois Byrnes (W. W. Norton and Company, 1978), p. 53; and *Collected Poems: 1930–1993*, p. 380.

p. 17   *The Silence Now: New and Uncollected Earlier Poems* (W. W. Norton and Company, 1988), p. 76 and *Collected Poems: 1930–1993*, p. 524.

pp. 20–21   *A Grain of Mustard Seed: New Poems* (W. W. Norton and Company, 1971), p. 43; and *Collected Poems: 1930–1993*, p. 343.

p. 25   *Mrs. Stevens Hears the Mermaids Singing: A Novel* (W. W. Norton and Company, 1965), p. 183.

p. 26   *Plant Dreaming Deep*, p. 94.

p. 28   *Plant Dreaming Deep* p. 70.

p. 30   *Plant Dreaming Deep*, p. 69 and *Recovering: A Journal*, pp. 32–33.

p. 31   *Journal of a Solitude*, pp. 19–196.

p. 31   *The House by the Sea*, p. 58.

p. 31   Ibid, p. 14.

p. 32   *Journal of a Solitude*, p. 11.

p. 33   *Plant Dreaming Deep*, p. 60.

p. 33   Ibid, p. 92.

p. 33   *Journal of a Solitude*, p. 94.

p. 33   Ibid, pp. 122–123.

p. 34   *After the Stroke: A Journal* (W. W. Norton and Company, 1988), p. 124.

p. 34   *Endgame: A Journal of the Seventy-ninth Year* (W. W. Norton and Company, 1992), p. 244.

p. 36   *Journal of a Solitude*, p. 57

pp. 38–41   *A Durable Fire*, pp. 11–14; *Selected Poems of May Sarton*, pp. 83–86; and *Collected Poems: 1930–1993*, pp. 367–370.

p. 43   *Journal of a Solitude*, p. 99.

p. 45   Ibid, p. 16.

p. 45   *Kinds of Love: A Novel* (W. W. Norton and Company, 1970), p. 93.

p. 46   *At Seventy: A Journal* (W. W. Norton and Company, 1984), p. 17.

p. 48   *Plant Dreaming Deep*, pp. 98–99.

p. 50   *As Does New Hampshire*, p. 25; and *Selected Poems of May Sarton*, p. 105; and *Collected Poems (1930–1993)*, p. 310.

p. 51   *A Grain of Mustard Seed*, p. 65; and *Collected Poems: 1930–1993*, p. 357.

p. 52   *Plant Dreaming Deep*, p. 100.

p. 54   *As Does New Hampshire*, p. 26; *Collected Poems: 1930–1993*, p. 311; and *Selected Poems of May Sarton*, p. 108.

p. 55   *A Durable Fire*, p. 22; *Collected Poems: 1930–1993*, p. 376.

p. 56   *Journal of a Solitude*, p. 11.

pp. 58–59   *Cloud , Stone, Sun, Vine*, pp. 140–141; and *Collected Poems: 1930–1993*, pp. 221–222.

p. 64   *Plant Dreaming Deep*, p. 125.

p. 64   *Journal of a Solitude*, p. 118.

p. 64   *Recovering: A Journal*, pp. 170–173.

p. 66   *Journal of a Solitude*, p. 34.

p. 68   *The House by the Sea*, p. 112.

p. 70   *A Durable Fire*, p. 32; and *Collected Poems: 1930–1993*, p. 383.

p. 71   *The Land of Silence* (Rinehart & Company, 1953), p. 34; and *Collected Poems: 1930–1993*, p. 145.

p. 72   *Plant Dreaming Deep*, p. 103.

p. 72   *The House by the Sea*, p. 52.

p. 74   *Recovering: A Journal*, p. 38.

p. 74   *The House by the Sea*, p. 52.

p. 76   *Letters from Maine*, p. 36; and *Collected Poems: 1930–1993*, p. 473.

p. 77   *Letters from Maine*, p. 31; and *Collected Poems: 1930–1993*, p. 469.

p. 78   *Joanna and Ulysses: A Tale* (W. W. Norton and Company, 1963 and 1991), p. 56.

pp. 80–81   *Coming into Eighty* (W. W. Norton and Company, 1994).

p. 85   *Mrs. Stevens Hears the Mermaids Singing*, p. 125.

p. 86   *A Grain of Mustard Seed*, p. 72; and *Collected Poems: 1930–1993*, p. 364.

p. 87   *The Silence Now*, p. 21; and *Collected Poems: 1930–1993*, p. 500.

p. 89   *Recovering: A Journal*, p. 115.

p. 90   *The Land of Silence*, p. 53; *Selected Poems of May Sarton*, p. 50; and *Collected Poems: 1930–1993*, p. 142.

p. 91   *Letters from Maine*, p. 48; and *Collected Poems: 1930–1993*, p. 481.

p. 93   *Endgame*, p. 166.

p. 94   *Recovering: A Journal*, p. 192.

pp. 96–97   *A Grain of Mustard Seed*, pp. 16–17; and *Selected Poems of May Sarton*, pp. 143–147.

p. 98   *The House by the Sea*, p. 25.

p. 98   Ibid, p. 23.

p. 98   *World of Light: A Portrait of May Sarton*, Produced and Directed by Marita Simpson and Martha Wheelock (Ishtar Films, 1979).

p. 100   *Recovering: A Journal*, p. 138

p. 100   Ibid, p. 205

p. 102   *Halfway to Silence: New Poems* (W. W. Norton and Company), p. 44; and *Collected Poems: 1930–1993*, p. 441.

p. 103   *A Grain of Mustard Seed*, p. 40; and *Collected Poems: 1930–1993*, p.340.

p. 107   *The Magnificent Spinster* (W. W. Norton and Company, 1985), p. 19.

p. 108   *The House by the Sea*, p. 255.

p. 111   *Recovering: A Journal*, pp. 202–203.

p. 111   *Journal of a Solitude*, p. 160.

p. 111   Ibid, p.56.

p. 111   *Recovering: A Journal*, p. 220.

P. 112   *Plant Dreaming Deep*, p. 87.

p. 114   *Journal of a Solitude*, p. 40

p. 116   *Recovering: A Journal*, p. 198

p. 116   *Journal of a Solitude*, p. 81.

p. 116   *The House by the Sea*, p. 177.

p. 116   *Recovering: A Journal*, p. 188.

p. 118   *Plant Dreaming Deep*, pp. 56–57

p. 120   *The Land of Silence*, p. 77; *Selected Poems of May Sarton*, p. 40; and *Collected Poems: 1930–1993*, p. 152.

p. 121   *In Time Like Air*, p. ; and *Collected Poems: 1930–1993*, p. 170.

p. 123   *At Seventy: A Journal*, p. 106.

p. 124   *The Inner Landscape*, p. ; and *Collected Poems: 1930–1993*, p. 37.

p. 125   *A Grain of Mustard Seed*, p. 36; and *Collected Poems: 1930–1993*, p. 337.

p. 127   *Journal of a Solitude*, p. 141.

p. 127   *Mrs. Stevens Hears the Mermaids Singing*, p. 191.

p. 127   *Plant Dreaming Deep*, p. 91.

p. 128   *Journal of a Solitude*, p. 67.

p. 130   *Recovering: A Journal*, p. 140.

p. 132   *Plant Dreaming Deep*, p.138.

pp. 134–135   *A Private Mythology: New Poems* (W. W. Norton and Company, 1966), pp. 103–104; and *Collected Poems: 1930–1993*, pp. 301–302.

p. 136   *At Seventy: A Journal*, p. 105.

p. 136   *Journal of a Solitude*, pp. 40–41.

p. 136   *Plant Dreaming Deep*, p. 151.

p. 138   *A Grain of Mustard Seed*, p. 51; and *Collected Poems: 1930–1993*, p. 348.

p. 139   *The Land of Silence*, p. 91; and *Collected Poems: 1930–1993*, p. 157.

Photograph References

Technical Notes

I primarily use 35mm cameras for my personal and creative work—a Nikon FM or FM2, with the recent addition of an 8008 to aid my aging eyes. I have 50mm, 55mm Macro, and 105mm lenses, plus 28-80 and 80-200mm zoom lenses. For commissioned photographs of people, or when I don't need to carry my camera too far, I use medium format Mamiya 645 cameras. I use 55mm, 80mm, or 150mm lenses for these cameras. I also use a tripod whenever time and circumstances allow it.

For many years I chose Kodak Plus X film, but I have recently switched to TMax 100. I continue to prefer Tri X film when I need more speed. I use TMax developer for TMax film and D76 developer with Tri X film (the same developer I previously used for Plus X film).

Since I develop and print my own black-and-white photographs, I have creative control during the entire photographic process. Generally my darkroom techniques are simple and straightforward—controlling contrast, burning and dodging a print to lighten and darken parts of it, or perhaps printing a negative backward to improve composition. There are times, however, when I turn to more involved techniques to create an image I envision. The photograph on page 131 (Peri Aston performing in "Dance of the Woman Warrior") is a montage: a print made from three different negatives on the same piece of paper. Unwanted parts of each image were masked during all or part of the exposure. In order to produce the blur in the photograph on page 112 (a kitchen counter), I moved the print (which I had placed on a lazy susan) during a fraction of the exposure.

Although I do work with color film, I find that black-and-white simplifies an image, giving emphasis to form and texture. Color often becomes too caught up with reality and dilutes the statement.

About Edith Royce Schade

Edith Royce Schade is a professional portrait and illustrative photographer. She has published her photographs in calendars, books, and magazines, and has exhibited in galleries in Connecticut. Ms. Schade has won several awards, including First Prize at the 1989 and 1990 Connecticut Audubon Society Photography Contest. Considering her camera an artistic tool, she uses photography to protect the environment and promote other civic causes. A native New Englander, Ms. Schade lives in Connecticut with her husband, a dog, a cat, a donkey, and numerous goats.

About May Sarton

May Sarton, born in Belgium and a long-time resident of New England, published her first poems at age seventeen. Ms. Sarton has published fifty-four volumes including poetry, novels, journals, essays, and children's books.

Papier-Mache Press

At Papier-Mache Press, it is our goal to identify and successfully present important social issues through enduring works of beauty, grace, and strength. Through our work we hope to encourage empathy and respect among diverse communities, creating a bridge of understanding between the mainstream audience and those who might not otherwise be heard.

We appreciate you, our customer, and strive to earn your continued support. We also value the role of the bookseller in achieving our goals. We are especially grateful to the many independent booksellers whose presence ensures a continuing diversity of opinion, information, and literature in our communities. We encourage you to support these bookstores with your patronage.

We publish many fine books about women's experiences. We also produce lovely posters and T-shirts that complement our anthologies. Please ask your local bookstore which Papier-Mache items they carry. To receive our complete catalog, send a self-addressed stamped envelope to Papier-Mache Press, 135 Aviation Way, #14, Watsonville, CA 95076, or call our toll-free number, 800-927-5913.